JACQUELINE MITTON holds an MA in Physics from the University of Oxford and a Doctorate in Astrophysics from the University of Cambridge. A prolific author of books and articles on astronomy, she has written or contributed to *The Young Oxford Book of Astronomy* (with husband Simon Mitton); *The Penguin Dictionary of Astronomy* and *The Concise Dictionary of Astronomy* (OUP); which was shortlisted for the Rhône Poulenc Junior Science Book Prize 1999. *Zoo in the Sky* was her first book for Frances Lincoln. Jacqueline lives in Cambridge.

CHRISTINA BALIT studied at Chelsea School of Art and the Royal College of Art. Her previous titles for Frances Lincoln include *Blodin the Beast* by Michael Morpurgo, which was shortlisted for the 1995 Kate Greenaway Medal; *Ishtar and Tammuz* by Christopher Moore, *Twelve Labours of Hercules* written by James Riordan, *Zoo in the Sky* by Jacqueline Mitton, *Women of Camelot* by Mary Hoffman, *Atlantis* and *My Sister Shahrazad* written by Robert Leeson. Christina lives in Kent with her family.

THE SMALL PLANETS

EARTH

PLUTO

MARS

MOON

8,000 km; 5,000 miles

VENUS

MERCURY

SUN

DEDICATED TO THE MEMORIES OF
FRANCES LINCOLN AND LUCY KEELING ✦ JM & CB

First published in Great Britain in 2001 by
Frances Lincoln Limited, 4 Torriano Mews,
Torriano Avenue, London NW5 2RZ
www.franceslincoln.com

First paperback edition 2003

British Library Cataloguing in Publication Data
available on request.

ISBN 0-7112-1947-8

Printed in Hong Kong

1 3 5 7 9 8 6 4 2

Kingdom of the Sun

A BOOK OF THE PLANETS

JACQUELINE MITTON • CHRISTINA BALIT

FRANCES LINCOLN

WE CAN BE PRETTY SURE that humans have always been sky watchers. Certainly, for many thousands of years people have followed the comings and goings of the Sun, the Moon and the five brightest planets – the ones we now call Mercury, Venus, Mars, Jupiter and Saturn.

THE WANDERERS

The English word 'planet' comes from the Greek word that means 'wanderer'. Ancient astronomers counted seven 'planets'. They included the Sun and Moon because they moved through the constellations. These astronomers also thought that the Earth was at the centre, with the seven 'planets' circling around it.

Today, by 'planet' we mean a world orbiting the Sun, or any other star. We know that the Moon travels around the Earth, and that the Sun is at the centre of a family of nine planets, including the Earth. Three of them were found only after the telescope was invented. Uranus was discovered in 1781, Neptune in 1846 and Pluto in 1930.

CITIZENS OF THE SUN'S KINGDOM

No-one really thinks there are more large planets in the Solar System waiting to be discovered, but there are many thousands of miniature planets. More of these are spotted every day. They are called asteroids, or sometimes minor planets. Most are concentrated in two ring-shaped belts around the Sun. One belt is between the orbits of Mars and Jupiter. The other lies just beyond Neptune and includes Pluto.

Altogether, the Sun rules over a huge population. This book is about the seven celestial 'wanderers' known to astronomers in ancient times, along with the three extra planets discovered since telescopes were invented – all objects that are visible in the night sky from Earth.

PLANETS AND GODS

About 2,300 years ago, the astronomer Aristotle gave the planets names of Greek gods. He followed the tradition of even earlier Babylonian astronomers who named the planets for their gods. Aristotle did his best to match the character the gods were supposed to have with what he knew about the planets – their speed, brightness and colour.

Later, Greek writing about the planets was translated into the Latin language, so the Greek planet names were changed to the names of the equivalent Roman gods. Hermes became Mercury, Aphrodite became Venus, Ares became Mars, Zeus became Jupiter and Cronus became Saturn. These are the names that have been handed down to us and are used by astronomers around the world today.

The Greeks also had a god and goddess to personify the Sun and Moon. Their names were Helios and Selene.

NAMING NEW PLANETS

When William Hershel discovered the planet Uranus in 1781, he wanted to name it in honour of the British King George III. In the end, the idea of calling it by the name of another god won out, and Uranus was selected. In one way, the pattern of planet names was broken though. Uranus is a Greek name. It was chosen because there is no Roman equivalent. The eighth planet to be found was named after Neptune, the Roman equivalent of the Greek god Poseidon. The Greek god Pluto gave his name to the ninth planet.

The people who named the planets knew little about them, but modern discoveries link with the old names in surprising ways. And though our knowledge of the Solar System has increased enormously since the ancient Greeks worshipped their gods, the sense of wonder about the planets is no less than it was all those centuries ago.

THE SUN

A MASSIVE BALL OF GLOWING FLAME, I am sovereign over nine planets. They speed around me along their orbits, trapped by the force of my gravity. Bathed in my rays, their faces beam brightly in the darkness of space.

At dawn I peep above Earth's horizon. I arise and lighten the daytime sky. I climb higher and higher till noon. In ancient Greece, people said I was like a god in a golden chariot, drawn through the heavens by fiery horses. Their name for me was Helios. After sunset they imagined me at rest, making ready for the next day's journey.

But I never rest! Ceaselessly I pour heat and light into the cold empty space about me. For I am a star, a fiery cosmic powerhouse. Billions of years have gone by since I first burst into light. Billions more will pass before I fade and die.

And I sit unmoved at the heart of my kingdom, the Solar System. Meanwhile, Earth spins and circles around me. It is you who are turning. My daily sky-ride is only an illusion.

THE MOON

POCKED WITH craters, pimpled with mountains, my lifeless face is stark and grey. I am no more than a ball of stone, circling the Earth month in and month out. But how do I appear in the clear night sky? I look neither drab nor ugly. Kissed by the rays of the Sun, my sombre rock is transmuted into beautiful shimmering silver.

Long ago I was seen as a goddess, Selene, sister of Helios the Sun. Gold and silver, we were a natural pair. His was the bright and cheery day, mine the secret shadowy night. The chariot to carry me through the sky was silver and my horses a pair of purest white.

Night by night, see how my appearance changes. As a slender crescent at dusk, I set soon after the Sun in the west. Within a week, half of me lights the evening hours. Wait seven more days and my whole round moon-face reflects sunlight over the dark Earth. After two weeks on the wane, I am a crescent once more. My cycle of transformation is complete.

MERCURY

CATCH ME IF YOU CAN as I dash around the Sun! My orbit almost hugs the Sun and I'm forced to lurk unseen in the dazzle of his brilliance. But now and again, for a mere few days, I dodge out of the glare to reveal where I am. And then you might spot me, very low in the twilight sky, shining as brightly as any star.

Swifter in motion than all other planets, I was given the name of Mercury, fleet-footed messenger of the gods and guardian of travellers. So nimble and cunning was he, no-one could catch him. With golden winged sandals upon his feet, he sped over land and sea like a breath of wind.

But no wind stirs on my bleak rocky surface. No atmosphere shields me from the blistering heat. From a pitch black sky, a huge Sun beats down in stillness on a myriad craters. Then after the Sun has gone down, a desperately chilly night follows each scorching day.

VENUS

A GLITTERING JEWEL OF THE HEAVENS, I blaze like a brilliant diamond. Matchless among the planets, I shine brighter than them all.

And my name I take from the love-goddess Venus, for her wondrous beauty outshone all her rivals. When three goddesses were judged to decide who was the fairest, she was awarded the prize – a golden apple.

No-one could fail to notice her. So when she wished to go unrecognised, she hid her face with a magical sparkling veil.

I too have a veil. Silvery cloudtops, glistening brightly in the Sun, always cover me with never a break. No telescope can see my naked face. And so, for many long years, I concealed my secrets.

But then came the spacecraft, armed with probes and radar beams. Now all is revealed. Fiery volcanoes have moulded features into my face unlike anything else in the Solar System. My atmosphere weighs down with almost incredible force. My world is seared by sweltering heat.

MARS

LIKE A FLAMING RUBY I burn in the night sky. They call me the Red Planet. Mine is the colour for anger and danger – the colour of blood.

Mars is the name I share with the god of war. Most feared of the gods, he was furious and fickle. He gloried in fighting and bloodshed. Fear and Terror were his constant companions. They follow me too, for my two tiny moons bear those names as the ancient Greeks would have said them – Phobos and Deimos.

But in truth I am a small and unthreatening world. My seasons come and go as on Earth. My only fury is the wind that blows wild and whips up rust-red dust till it fills the thin air and billows for mile upon mile. Travel back in time, though, and you would see me differently. Towering volcanoes, long since extinct, are silent witnesses to my violent past. Winding channels scar me where torrents of water once swept by. But that was billions of years ago. Dry, shifting sand is all that moves on Mars today.

JUPITER

I AM THE GREATEST of the Sun's planets. My bulk surpasses a thousand Earths. My radiance makes me a beacon of the night – brilliant, yellow and steadfast. A retinue of twenty-eight moons or more revolves around me, caught in my gravity's power.

It is fitting that I am called Jupiter, named for the greatest of the gods who ruled supreme among them all. Clouds and rain were his special charge, thunder and lightning signs of his anger.

Clouds are my glory too, swirling, whirling, and weaving intricate patterns. And flashing through my stormy weather, immense electric sparks inject my clouds with jagged lightning. My most enormous storm of all has raged for hundreds of years, spiralling wildly. Called the Great Red Spot, it could cover several Earths.

Plunge below my restless kaleidoscope of clouds and you would find an unimaginably strange world where thick gas blends little by little into liquid. Venture deeper into my globe, and encounter a metallic liquid like nothing known on Earth.

SATURN

WHAT A GLORIOUS ARRAY OF RINGS and moons surrounds me! I preside over a wealth of plenty, as Saturn the god did in the Golden Age when he reigned. My rings are shoals of countless scurrying moonlets, casting a multicoloured girdle about my belly. Braiding and streaming, clustering here, dividing there, they whirl by in a frenzy. Some are icy boulders the size of a castle. The smallest are mere specks of dust. My real moons – those large enough to have their own names – number at least thirty.

My namesake among the gods was once ruler of them all. But he yielded to Jupiter, his mightier son, who banished him afar into the heavens. Indeed, I am almost double Jupiter's distance from the Sun. By size I rank close second to him.

A veil of haze makes my creamy clouds look calm. But things are not always as they seem. High-speed winds race around my spinning globe. Now and again, a giant storm breaks out, topped by a dramatic white cloud.

URANUS

AN ORB OF PALE AND GENTLE BLUE, with scarcely a feature to show, I wend my way around the Sun in the distant reaches of the Solar System. With my heavenly colour, I am fittingly named as the sky god of old. Husband of Mother Earth, he was father to Saturn, and Jupiter was his grandson.

Set four Earths side by side to gauge my size. Though I have a rocky core, my main bulk is a curious chemical sea, with hazy atmosphere above. Clouds are rare and I am indeed plain and bland. Some declare me dull. Yet I have a little mystery. As I voyage on my path through space, I roll along upon my side, axis askew. What happened in the dim and distant past to cause me to tumble so?

A swarm of little moons buzzes around me. Astronomers have counted twenty-one. My nine fine rings of flying boulders are dim and dark – dark as anything in the Sun's whole realm.

NEPTUNE

THROUGH THE DEPTHS OF SPACE I sail my course around the Sun, six times farther off than Jupiter. My face is bright blue, the colour of Earth's ocean. My name I take from the god of the seas, Jupiter's powerful, bad-tempered brother. With a shake of his three-pronged trident he could summon a storm at will. And he rode the surf in a chariot pulled by magical serpent horses.

Like the white foam horses atop tumbling waves, ice-crystal clouds form glistening froth upon me. They gallop along, tossed by the fiercest winds known on any planet, then they vanish into the blue. Once in a while, brooding storms blow up in writhing oval spots of darker hue.

Though I am named as Jupiter's brother, by nature Uranus is my closest kin. Like him I'm surrounded by thin dusky rings, though one of mine is a broken chain of curving arcs. Two blue giants, we make a pair as large as each other. But Uranus is serene while I am wild and tempestuous.

PLUTO

AT THE FAR-FLUNG EDGE of the Sun's domain, chilled almost to the deepest cold that ever can be, I hold my moon Charon close. Two miniature worlds of ice and rock, we circle each other face-to-face. The sunbeams that reach me are weak after travelling so very far. Darkness envelops me, like the gloom in the caverns of the underworld where Pluto the god reigned. His was the realm of the souls of the dead and Charon was the boatman who ferried them there.

All around me, thousands of icy bodies wander through space like ghosts. These dwarf planets accompany me on centuries-long loops around the Solar System, where Neptune lies and beyond. My oval course sometimes swings me as near as Neptune, sometimes carries me much farther off. Because I am so far away and tiny – less than one fifth of Earth's span – vague shadowy patches are all that can be seen of me, though telescopes strain their best. No spacecraft has yet been my way to snatch a close-up of my face.

MORE ABOUT THE SUN, MOON AND PLANETS

PLANET NAME	AVERAGE DISTANCE FROM SUN	DIAMETER AT EQUATOR	TIME TO ORBIT SUN	NUMBER OF MOONS
MERCURY	58 million km (36 million miles)	4,878 km (3,031 miles)	88.0 days	0
VENUS	108 million km (67 million miles)	12,104 km (7,521 miles)	224.7 days	0
EARTH	150 million km (93 million miles)	12,756 km (7,926 miles)	1.00 year	1
MARS	228 million km (142 million miles)	6,794 km (4,222 miles)	1.88 years	2
JUPITER	778 million km (483 million miles)	143,884 km (89,408 miles)	11.86 years	28
SATURN	1,427 million km (887 million miles)	120,536 km (74,898 miles)	29.46 years	30
URANUS	2,871 million km (1,784 million miles)	51,118 km (31,765 miles)	84.01 years	21
NEPTUNE	4,497 million km (2,794 million miles)	6,794 km (4,222 miles)	164.79 years	8
PLUTO	5,914 million km (3,675 million miles)	2,360 km (1,466 miles)	248 years	1

Mercury, Venus and Mars are small rocky planets like Earth. The Moon is like a small rocky planet too. The four giant planets – Jupiter, Saturn, Uranus and Neptune – have rocky cores, but there is no solid surface below their atmospheres. Instead, the gas gets thicker the farther you go down until it merges into a very deep layer of liquid. Tiny Pluto is different again, made of a mixture of ice and rock.

ABOUT THE SUN

- 109 times larger than Earth
- 333,000 times more massive than Earth
- 15 million °C at the centre
- 5,500 °C at the surface

ABOUT THE MOON

- Diameter 3,476 km (2,160 miles)
- Average distance from Earth 384,400 km (238,861 miles)
- Takes 27.32 days to spin once
- There are 29.53 days between new Moons

GLOSSARY

ASTRONOMER – Someone who studies the universe
and the things in it, such as stars and planets.

ATMOSPHERE – A layer of gas around a moon,
planet or star.

CONSTELLATION – A named area of sky and the
pattern of stars in it.

COSMIC – To do with space or the universe.

CRATER – A bowl-shaped hole in the surface of a
moon or planet.

GRAVITY – A natural force that makes objects attract
each other.

HORIZON – Where the sky seems to meet
the ground.

MOON – A body that moves in orbit around
a planet.

MOONLET – A very small moon.

ORBIT – The path in space of one body around
another; to travel around another body.

PLANET – A world that, unlike a star, is not massive
enough to give out any light of its own.

PROBE – A spacecraft sent to investigate the atmosphere
or surface of a planet or moon, by dropping through
the atmosphere or landing on the surface.

RADAR – A way of finding out the distance to
something by bouncing radio waves from it.

SOLAR SYSTEM – All the things in orbit around
the Sun that are kept there by the Sun's gravity,
including the planets with their moons, comets
and asteroids.

STAR – A large glowing ball of hot gas.

VOLCANO – A mountain formed where molten rock
has welled up to the surface from the inside of a planet.

THE GIANT PLANETS

URANUS

SIZE OF EARTH

JUPITER

80,000 km; 50,000 miles

NEPTUNE

SATURN

SUN

MORE PICTURE BOOKS IN PAPERBACK FROM FRANCES LINCOLN

ZOO IN THE SKY

Jacqueline Mitton

Illustrated by Christina Balit

Drawing on the fascination of the heavens, this introduction to the night sky, stars and galaxies includes maps of the Southern and Northern skies charting the history of the constellations and the Milky Way.

Suitable for National Curriculum English – Reading, Key Stage 1 and 2
Scottish Guidelines English Language – Reading, Level C

ISBN 0-7112-1319-4

THE TWELVE LABOURS OF HERCULES

James Riordan

Illustrated by Christina Balit

James Riordan's bold retellings of the ancient Greek legends recreate the astonishing feats of strength carried out by Zeus' much-loved son and mythology's mightiest hero, in a powerfully illustrated anthology that children will reach for again and again.

Suitable for National Curriculum English – Reading, Key Stage 2 and 3
Scottish Guidelines English Language – Reading, Levels D and E

ISBN 0-7112-1391-7

ATLANTIS
LEGEND OF A LOST CITY

Christina Balit

When Poseidon marries a beautiful mortal named Cleito, he transforms her island into a rich, fertile place where he builds a perfect city and names it Atlantis. But as the years pass, his descendants start to act less like gods and more like men. With a note by Geoffrey Ashe, this retelling echoes one of the most haunting themes of humankind.

Suitable for National Curriculum English – Reading, Key Stage 2; History, Key Stage 2
Scottish Guidelines English Language – Reading, Level C

ISBN 0-7112-1906-0

Frances Lincoln titles are available from all good bookshops.
You can also buy books and find out more about your favourite titles, authors and illustrators at our website: www.franceslincoln.com.